UNDERSTANDING**SCIENCE**

GRAVITY

PUBLISHED BY SMART APPLE MEDIA
1980 Lookout Drive, North Mankato, Minnesota 56003

PHOTOGRAPHS by Richard Cummins, Galyn C. Ham-
mond, Tom Myers, NASA, Tom Pantages (NASA),
Photri-Microstock (Scott Berner), Tom Stack & Asso-
ciates (John Gerlach, NASA/JPL/TSADO, Greg Vaughn),
Unicorn Stock Photos (Jeff Greenberg, R. J. Mathews)

DESIGN AND PRODUCTION Evansday Design

LIBRARY OF CONGRESS CATALOGING-IN-PUBLICATION DATA

Tiner, John Hudson, 1944–
Gravity / by John Hudson Tiner.
p. cm. — (Understanding science)
Includes index.

Summary: Presents information on the scientific
principle of gravity, how it was discovered, and how
knowledge of its effect is applied by astronomers.
Includes directions for a simple experiment.

ISBN 1-58340-157-1

1. Gravity—Juvenile literature. [1. Gravity.] I. Title. II.
Understanding science (North Mankato, Minn.).

QC178.T53 2002

531'.14—dc21   2001054153

First Edition

9 8 7 6 5 4 3 2 1

Gravity

UNDERSTANDING SCIENCE

[John Hudson Tiner]

A YOUNG CHILD LEARNING TO WALK SOON BECOMES AWARE OF GRAVITY. THE CHILD ALWAYS FALLS DOWN AND NEVER FALLS UP. GRAVITY IS ALWAYS PULLING ON US AND EVERYTHING AROUND US. A BASEBALL STRUCK BY A BAT ALWAYS RETURNS TO EARTH BECAUSE OF GRAVITY, AND GRAVITY CONTROLS THE PATH OF THE MOON AS IT ORBITS AROUND EARTH. THE STORY OF HOW SCIENTISTS FOUND OUT ABOUT GRAVITY IS AN EXCITING ONE.

In the late 1960s and early '70s, America's Apollo space program sent the first human beings to the moon. David Scott was one of the *Apollo 15* astronauts who landed on the moon in 1971. While on the moon's surface, Scott did an unusual **experiment**. He held a falcon feather in his left hand. In his right hand, he held a hammer. Scott let go of the hammer and feather at the same moment. On Earth, the feather would have floated down because of the air. But the moon has no atmosphere. Without air to slow the feather, the feather fell at the same speed as the hammer. They descended side by side and hit the moon's surface at the same time. To people watching by television, Scott said, "Galileo, a long time ago, made an important discovery about falling objects in gravity fields." Galileo Galilei was an Italian scientist who lived 400 years ago. Scientists of Galileo's day believed

An **experiment** *is a test in a controlled setting, such as a science lab-oratory, conducted to learn about a subject.*

THE APOLLO MOON LANDINGS ILLUSTRATED THE EFFECTS OF GRAVITY

A person can learn the depth of a well by dropping in a pebble. The number of seconds until the splash tells the distance to the water: one second = 16 feet (4.9 m), two seconds = 64 feet (19.5 m), and three seconds = 144 feet (43.9 m).

GALILEO IS SAID TO HAVE CONDUCTED TESTS FROM THE LEANING TOWER OF PISA

A **pendulum** is a weight held from a string or chain that
swings freely to and fro because of gravity.

that heavy objects fell faster than light ones. They said that a ball 10 times as heavy as another ball would fall 10 times as fast. Around 1589, a rumor sprang up that Galileo tested this claim. According to the rumor, Galileo one day dropped two iron balls of different sizes from the Leaning Tower of Pisa. One ball was light, and the other one was heavy. Both struck the ground at the same time. This experiment may not have taken place. But for 18 years, Galileo did other gravity experiments. He learned that a falling object picked up speed each

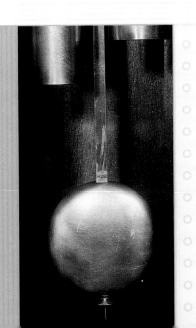

Galileo timed the motion of a **pendulum**. He proved that all pendulums of the same length swing at the same rate regardless of weight. The motion is so regular that it can keep time. A grandfather clock is a pendulum clock.

second that it fell. An iron ball took one second to fall 16 feet (4.9 m), but at the end of that second it was falling 32 feet (9.8 m) per second. Galileo gave the name **acceleration** to the gain in speed. His experiments showed that the acceleration due to gravity is 32 feet (9.8 m) per second every second. If air did not slow it down, a falling object would accelerate at this rate until it struck the surface of the earth. Galileo tested objects made of wood, glass, lead, and many other materials. He discovered that gravity caused all of them to fall at the

Galileo was the first person to view the night sky with a telescope. He discovered four moons revolving around Jupiter. Jupiter's gravity carried the moons with it during its journey around the sun.

GALILEO ESTABLISHED THE FOUNDATION OF OUR KNOWLEDGE OF GRAVITY

same speed. Without air to slow it, Galileo claimed, a feather would fall at the same speed as a lump of lead. However, he could not try this experiment because an air pump for removing air from a container had not yet been invented.

In 1665, Isaac Newton attended college in Cambridge, England. Because of an outbreak of the Black Death, a terrible **plague**, the students were sent home. While at home, Newton set up a study table in an apple orchard. One day, an apple fell from a tree and banged on his table. As Newton held the apple, he noticed the rising moon. He knew that gravity pulled the apple toward the earth. But he wondered if gravity extended into space. Could gravity hold the moon in **orbit** around the earth? The moon's path constantly curved as if an invisible cord held it to the center of the earth. Newton believed that this cord was the pull of gravity. Gravity did not change the speed of the moon as it traveled through space. But it did change the direction the moon traveled. Changing direction is also a type of acceleration. Newton knew that the

*A **plague** is a widespread and highly infectious disease that is often fatal.*

*An **orbit** is the path of an object as it revolves around another object.*

EARTH PULLS ON THE MOON FROM 240,000 MILES (386,400 KM) AWAY

A tide is a change in the level of the ocean. Isaac Newton was the first person to explain that tides are the effect of the gravitational attraction of the moon and sun upon the waters of Earth.

Squared in mathematics means to multiply a number by itself; for example, four is two squared.

SHUTTLES NEED TREMENDOUS FUEL PROPULSION TO ESCAPE EARTH'S GRAVITY

moon was 60 times farther from the center of the earth than the apple was. When he calculated the acceleration of the moon, he found it to be 3,600 times less than the acceleration of the apple. This number is 60 **squared**: 60 x 60 = 3,600. Newton

Escape velocity is the speed an object must have to break away from the gravitational attraction of a planet.

said that gravity grew weaker by the square of the distance. For example, an apple at the top of a 4,000 mile (6,437 km) high tree would be twice as far from the center of the earth as an apple in an ordinary tree. Gravity on an apple twice as far away would be four times weaker: 2 x 2 = 4. As a rocket travels away from Earth, the planet's gravitational pull on the rocket gets weaker. Gravity never goes away entirely. But a rocket going 25,000 miles (40,200 km) per hour will never fall back to Earth. This speed is known as the **escape velocity** from Earth.

Galileo was born the same year (1564) that the great artist Michelangelo died. Galileo died the same year (1642) that Isaac Newton was born. Newton was born on Christmas Day.

The fact that gravity grows weaker on objects with the square of the distance was an important discovery. But Newton was not finished studying gravity. He gave the name **force** to a push or pull. Gravitational attraction is the force that pulls all objects to Earth, including the apple. **Weight** is a measure of the force of gravitational attraction. Objects weigh less wherever the force of gravity is weaker. Gravity on the moon is not as strong as gravity on Earth. The same object is therefore lighter on the moon than it is on Earth. For instance, astronaut David Scott drove a battery-powered cart around on the moon. On Earth, the *Lunar Rover* weighed 622 pounds (282 kg). On the moon, it weighed 104 pounds (47 kg). Weight can change from one place to another. The **mass** of an object, however, stays the same everywhere. Mass is an-

The **Lunar Rover** *was a four-wheeled, battery-powered vehicle used by Apollo astronauts to explore the moon's surface.*

A **force** is a push or pull upon an object; the force of gravity pulls objects to the earth.

Weight is a measure of the force of gravity on an object.

AN ASTRONAUT OPERATING THE LUNAR ROVER ON THE MOON'S SURFACE

A person who weighs 90 pounds (41 kg) on Earth would weigh 30 pounds (13.6 kg) on the planet Mars and 225 pounds (102 kg) on Jupiter. Mars has less mass than Earth, while Jupiter has greater mass than Earth.

other term that Newton defined. Mass is the amount of material in an object. Even floating weightless in space, an apple has the same mass as it has on Earth. The force of gravity depends on the mass of an object. A greater mass produces a greater force of gravity. Any two objects attract one another. Two apples sitting on a table attract one another, but because their masses are so small, the force is too slight to cause them to roll together. The earth and an apple attract one another. The mass of the earth is great enough to cause the apple to fall to the earth. The apple attracts the earth,

The English astronomer Edmund Halley was a friend of Isaac Newton. Halley used the law of gravity to predict the return of a **comet**. The comet did return, just as Halley predicted. It became known as Halley's Comet.

THE MORE MASSIVE A PLANET, THE GREATER ITS PULL ON SPACECRAFT

A **comet** is a ball of gas and dust that grows a glowing tail as it passes near the sun.

*The **universe** is everything in existence from the center of the earth to the farthest reaches of space.*

NOTHING IN THE KNOWN UNIVERSE CAN ESCAPE THE EFFECTS OF GRAVITY

too. But the mass of the apple is very slight. Its gravity does not affect the earth in any way that can be measured. The moon, however, does have enough mass to affect the earth. The moon doesn't merely circle the earth; the earth and the moon circle around one another. Because of the earth's greater mass, it moves much less than the moon

*The **product** is the quantity or number obtained by multiplying two or more numbers together.*

does. Newton also said that the law of gravity applies to every object in the **universe**. Grains of sand and distant stars all follow the law of gravity. The law of gravity states that the force of attraction between two objects is equal to the **product** of their masses divided by the square of the distance between their centers. Simply put, this means gravity between two objects grows weaker if they are placed farther apart from one another, but grows stronger if one or the other is replaced by a more massive object.

Although Newton was one of the greatest scientists who ever lived, he gave credit for his success to others before him. Newton once said, "If I have seen farther it is because I have stood on the shoulders of giants."

For many years, Uranus was the farthest known planet from the sun. Because of the great distance between the sun and Uranus, the force of gravity between the two is weak. Uranus moves slowly. It takes 84 Earth years for Uranus to go around the sun once. All of the planets orbit the sun because the sun has a mass far greater than all of their masses combined. The planet Uranus was discovered in 1781. Forty years later, astronomers saw that Uranus had strayed from its predicted path. George Airy was the chief astronomer in England at the time. He claimed that the law of gravity broke down at great distances from the sun. In 1843, John Coach Adams was a young mathematics student in Cambridge, England. He disagreed with Airy and suspected that the pull of gravity from an unseen planet was dragging Uranus off course. Adams set out to find the mystery planet. Rather

WITH 318 TIMES THE MASS OF EARTH, JUPITER HAS POWERFUL GRAVITY

Jupiter is the largest planet in our solar system. The planet is large enough to cause the sun to wobble. If astronomers were on nearby stars, they would be able to see the wobble caused by Jupiter.

than looking through a telescope, he used a pen and paper. Based on the changes in the orbit of Uranus, he calculated where the other planet must be. It took him two years, but in 1845, Adams had the position of the mystery planet. Adams was excited about his discovery. He visited George Airy's home and knocked on his door. He planned to ask Airy to look for the planet. However, the astronomer was too busy to talk with the young student and sent Adams away. Adams did leave his report behind, but Airy tossed it aside and did not look for the planet. Several months later, a well-known French astronomer named Joseph Le Ver-

In *Principia*, Newton's book about gravity, he suggested that an object could be put into orbit around the earth. However, it wasn't until the 1950s that rockets were powerful enough to carry **artificial satellites** into space.

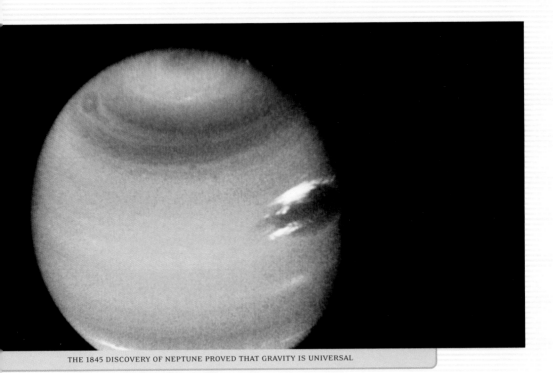

THE 1845 DISCOVERY OF NEPTUNE PROVED THAT GRAVITY IS UNIVERSAL

rier made the same calculations and arrived at the same answer as Adams. He asked German astronomer Johann Galle to look for the planet. That night, the astronomer began the search. Within 30 minutes, Galle spied the new planet. It had a sea-green color, and was named Neptune after the Roman god of the sea. The discovery of Neptune by pen-and-paper calculations put to rest any doubts about Newton's law of gravity. Adams and Le Verrier proved that it held true even at great distances from the sun.

In the 1600s, scientists learned that stars are large, glowing objects like the sun but very far away. Since then, scientists have wondered if other stars have planets like those that orbit the sun. Stars are enormous, but they are so far away that most just look like points of light when viewed through even the most powerful telescopes. Planets would be even smaller, and impossible to see directly. Despite the difficulty, astronomers have discovered planets orbiting other suns. The first was discovered in 1992. In the next 10 years, astronomers found about 60 more planets in orbit around distant stars. These hidden planets are revealed by the wobble they cause in the stars they orbit. Stars travel through space, and powerful telescopes reveal this motion. But some stars are pulled from their straight course by objects orbiting them. Some of these unseen companions are very dim

WOBBLING STARS ALLOW US TO SEE GRAVITY AT WORK LIGHT-YEARS AWAY

Some stars are so massive that the escape velocity from them is faster than the speed of light. Light itself cannot escape from them, and they appear dark. For that reason, these very massive stars are known as black holes.

WITHOUT GRAVITY TO HOLD EARTH'S ELEMENTS TOGETHER, LIFE COULD NOT EXIST

stars. But others are too small to be stars. They must be planets. As a planet orbits a star, the planet's gravity pulls the star first one way and then the other. Much still remains to be learned about gravity. Gravity is one of the most important forces of nature. The hot gases that make up the sun are held in place by gravity. Without gravity, these gases would escape into space, and the sun would burn out. Likewise, a bit of sand on a beach is held in place by gravity. Without gravity, the rapidly spinning Earth would come apart. Everything—buildings, mountains, and people—would be tossed into space. Gravity is the force that holds the universe together.

GALILEO USED PENDULUMS EXTENSIVELY TO TEST THE EFFECTS OF GRAVITY

A pendulum is a string, stick, or metal rod with a weight on it that swings back and forth because of the pull of gravity. In this experiment, you will make pendulums of various substances and test the effect of gravity on them.

WHAT YOU NEED

String

A tape measure

A ruler

A stack of books

A small plastic sandwich bag

A glass marble, metal bolt, wooden block, and coins

WHAT YOU DO

1. Set the ruler so one end extends over the edge of a table; hold the other end down with a stack of books.

2. Place a glass marble in the plastic bag and tie it to one end of the string.

3. Adjust the string so the distance from the center of the glass marble to the ruler is 24 inches (61 cm). Tie the string to the ruler.

4. Pull the weight two or three inches (5–7.5 cm) to one side and release it.

5. Count the number of complete swings (back and forth) in one minute; write down this number.

6. Repeat steps two through five with the other weights.

WHAT YOU SEE

In one minute, a pendulum of wood, glass, metal, or any other material makes the same number of swings. The pendulum swings because of the acceleration of gravity. As Galileo showed, the acceleration of gravity is the same regardless of the weight of the object or the material that makes it.

INDEX